Language Literacy Lessons

Reading

Intermediate Grades

by Imogene Forte

Incentive Publications, Inc.
Nashville, Tennessee

Illustrated by Gayle S. Harvey
Cover Art by Rebecca Rüegger
Edited by Jean K. Signor

ISBN 0-86530-570-6

PRINTED IN THE UNITED STATES OF AMERICA
www.incentivepublications.com

Table of Contents

Appendix 71

HOW TO USE THIS BOOK

Achieving language literacy is a major benchmark in the education of every student in today's classrooms. Without reading, writing, speaking, and listening literacy the process of learning becomes increasingly difficult and the limits placed on academic achievement become more entrenched and solidified each year.

In the information saturated and technology dependent world of today, it is especially important for children to gain and be able to make meaningful use of the skills associated with language literacy at an early age. Success in content-based studies such as Math, Social Studies, and Science, and even in enrichment fields including Art, Music, and Literature are highly dependent on language literacy proficiency. With strong language skills, a student's academic future has fewer bounds and individual goals, expectancies and dreams stand a better chance of being realized. It was with respect for the importance of achieving a high level of language literacy for every student that the Language Literacy Lessons Series was developed.

The purpose of *Language Literacy Lessons: Reading, Intermediate* is to help students achieve the desired literacy milestone through reinforcement of key language skills. The activities in this book have all been designed to provide student practice of essential reading skills. A skills checklist on page 10 details the skills covered. This skills checklist has been carefully gleaned from attention to research related to language, while specific skills associated with each lesson are correlated to the age-appropriate language literacy checklist.

Through the use of the lessons in this book, students will be advancing individual language literacy skills while working toward national standards! For help in lesson planning, an easy-to-use matrix on pages 8 and 9 presents National Language Arts Standards correlations for each lesson in the book.

Not only are the activities correlated to essential literacy skills and National Language Arts Standards, they are imaginative and their open-ended nature will prove to be engaging and of high-interest to students. Student creativity is tapped through intriguing situations to write about, interesting characters to read about, and captivating illustrations to inspire thoughtful student responses.

As language literacy skills improve, increased levels of overall school success will be readily apparent. Language literacy enables students to set achievable goals to go wherever their interests take them and to embark joyfully on a lifelong journey of learning!

STANDARDS MATRIX

STANDARD	ACTIVITY PAGE
Standard 1: Students read a wide range of print and nonprint text to build an understanding of texts, of themselves, and of the cultures of the United States and the world, to acquire new information, to respond to the needs and demands of society and the workplace, and for personal fulfillment. Among these texts are fiction and nonfiction, classic and contemporary works.	24, 27, 30, 34, 46, 64-65
Standard 2: Students read a wide range of literature from many periods in many genres to build an understanding of the many dimensions (e.g., philosophical, ethical, aesthetic) of human experience.	31, 32, 38, 39
Standard 3: Students apply a wide range of strategies to comprehend, interpret, evaluate, and appreciate texts. They draw on their prior experience, their interactions with other readers and writers, their knowledge of word meaning and of other texts, their identification strategies, and their understanding of textual features (e.g., sound-letter correspondence, sentence structure, context, graphics).	16, 17, 19, 52-53, 56, 68
Standard 4: Students adjust their use of spoken, written, and visual language (e.g., conventions, style, vocabulary) to communicate effectively with a variety of audiences for a variety of purposes.	18, 20, 26, 54, 60, 67
Standard 5: Students employ a wide range of strategies as they write and use different writing process elements appropriately to communicate with different audiences for a variety of purposes.	21, 48, 66
Standard 6: Students apply knowledge of language structure, language conventions (e.g., spelling and punctuation), media techniques, figurative language, and genre to create, critique, and discuss print and non-print texts.	12, 13, 14, 15, 61

Standards for the English Language Arts, by the International Reading Association and the National Council of Teachers of English, Copyright 1996 by the International Reading Association and the National Council of Teachers of English. Reprinted with permission.

Language Literacy Lessons / Reading Intermediate

STANDARDS MATRIX

STANDARD	ACTIVITY PAGE
Standard 7: Students conduct research on issues and interests by generating ideas and questions, and by posing problems. They gather, evaluate, and synthesize data from a variety of sources (e.g., print and non-print texts, artifacts, people) to communicate their discoveries in ways that suit their purpose and audience.	23, 25, 35, 36, 57, 72
Standard 8: Students use a variety of technological and informational resources (e.g., libraries, databases, computer networks, video) to gather and synthesize information and to create and communicate knowledge.	33, 45, 59, 62
Standard 9: Students develop an understanding of and respect for diversity in language use, patterns, and dialects across cultures, ethnic groups, geographic regions, and social roles.	37, 41-43, 58
Standard 10: Students whose first language is not English make use of their first language to develop competency in the English language arts and to develop understanding of content across the curriculum.	40, 47, 50
Standard 11: Students participate as knowledgeable, reflective, creative, and critical members of a variety of literacy communities.	28, 44, 51, 55, 69, 70
Standard 12: Students use spoken, written, and visual language to accomplish their own purposes (e.g., for learning, enjoyment, persuasion, and the exchange of information).	22, 49, 63, 74, 75

Language Literacy Lessons / Reading Intermediate   *Standards for the English Language Arts,* by the International Reading Association and the National Council of Teachers of English, Copyright 1996 by the International Reading Association and the National Council of Teachers of English. Reprinted with permission.

SKILLS CHECKLIST

√	SKILL	PAGE
	Recognizes Consonants and Vowels	12
	Knows and Can Use Prefixes	13
	Knows and Can Use Suffixes	14
	Can Use Contractions	15
	Can Use Abbreviations	16
	Can Use Compound Words	17
	Can Use Picture Clues	18, 40, 47
	Can Use Context Clues	19, 27, 67
	Recognizes and Can Use Antonyms	20
	Recognizes and Can Use Homonyms	21
	Recognizes and Can Use Synonyms	22
	Can Form Sensory Impressions	23
	Can Use Figurative Language	24, 25
	Can Interpret Idiomatic Expressions	26
	Descriptive Words	27
	Demonstrates Vocabulary Extension Skills	28
	Can Read for a Specific Purpose	30
	Can Identify Topic Sentences	31
	Can Read to Find Details	32, 33, 34
	Can Arrange Ideas or Events in Sequence	35, 36
	Can Summarize	37, 38, 39
	Can Draw Conclusions	40
	Can Read and Use a World Map	41–42
	Can Predict Outcomes	43, 44
	Distinguishing Between Fact and Opinion	45, 46
	Can Distinguish Between Cause and Effect	47
	Is Sensitive to Author's Purpose and Mood	48
	Can Identify with Fictional Characters	49, 50, 51
	Can Visualize Word Meaning	54, 55
	Can Alphabetize	56
	Can Determine What Reference Source to Use, and Can Use Multiple Resources	57, 58
	Can Use the Thesaurus or Encyclopedia	59, 60
	Can Understand and Use Punctuation	61
	Can Follow Written Directions	62, 63, 64, 65
	Can Take Notes from Reading	66
	Can Organize Facts to Support a Conclusion	67
	Is Developing Appreciation and Reading Independence	52-53, 68, 69, 70

Word Recognition and Usage Skills

The Missing Monarch

Find the beautiful monarch butterfly that is trapped in this picture by coloring all spaces containing the letters in the word "butterfly."

Use your colored pencils to color the spaces containing consonants orange and the spaces containing vowels black.

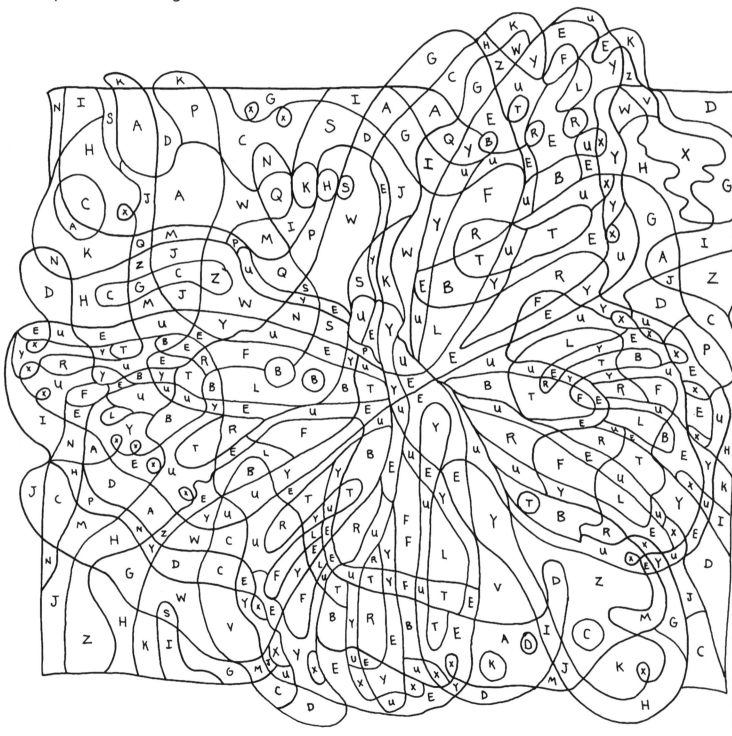

Name: _____

Date: _____

Recognizing Consonants and Vowels

Language Literacy Lessons / Reading Intermediate
Copyright ©2002 by Incentive Publications, Inc.
Nashville, TN.

Prefix Pyramids

Long ago in the Egyptian desert, the famous Pyramids of the Pharaohs were built.

You, too, can be a pyramid builder. Select words from the root word list below to add to the prefix at the top of each empty pyramid.

Begin at the bottom of each pyramid and work toward the top.

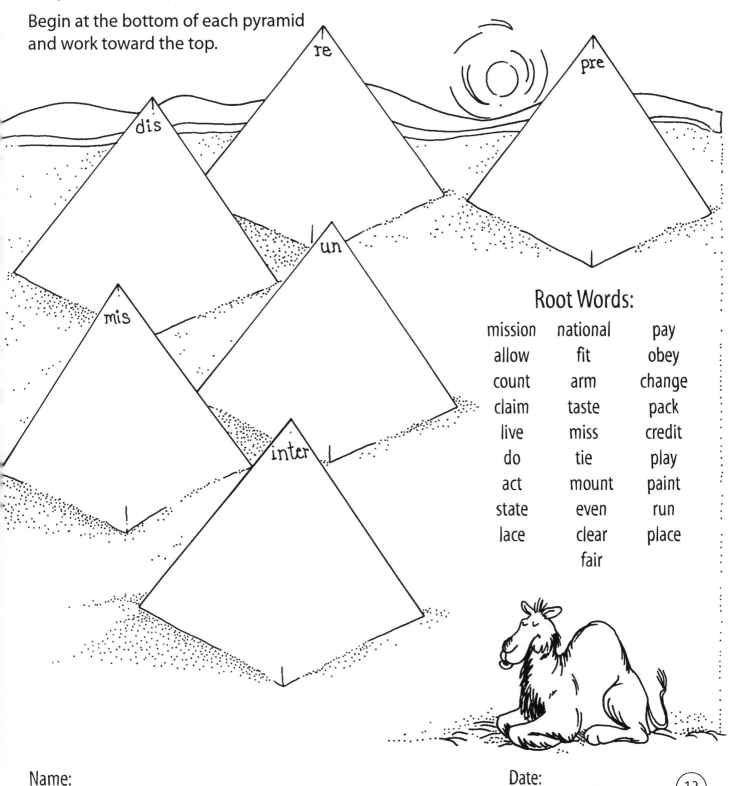

Root Words:

mission	national	pay
allow	fit	obey
count	arm	change
claim	taste	pack
live	miss	credit
do	tie	play
act	mount	paint
state	even	run
lace	clear	place
	fair	

Suffixes for the Sorcerer

This sorcerer is trying to make a name for himself by adding new words to the Sorcerer Society's Suffix Bag.

Help him by dipping into the word pool for words to add to the suffixes.

Write them in their proper places on the suffix bag to make new words.

grace   good

pay   friend

fool   help

act   patient

search

teach

deep

art

interest

_____ed

_____ive   _____ist

_____est   _____ful

_____ish   _____er

_____ly   _____ing

_____ship   _____ness

_____ment   _____less

Date: _____

The Mermaid's Tale

Underline the phrase or phrases in each group that contain a contraction.

Circle the phrase or phrases in each group that contain an apostrophe to show possession.

1. The mermaid's fins
   She doesn't know
   The ocean's floor

2. The waves' roar
   They can't hear
   It wasn't safe

3. Shouldn't she go
   Her mother's party
   She'll know soon

4. The boat's sail
   I'm interested
   Here's another story

5. She'll tell me
   I'll never tell
   The sea's secrets

6. There's a treasure somewhere
   They'll keep searching
   The diver's work

7. She didn't remember
   Her friend's message
   It's getting late

8. The sailor's question
   Merry's answer
   The tale's almost told

9. Here's the chest
   The gold's glitter
   You've guessed the secret

10. Gus couldn't swim
    Geneva's blonde hair
    Glen's laughter

11. The bottle's message
    Who's there
    The sea's song

12. Romeo's ready
    It's never too late
    Julie's story

Name:

Date:

Language Literacy Lessons / Reading Intermediate
Copyright ©2002 by Incentive Publications, Inc.
Nashville, TN.

Using Contractions

A Short Letter

Humberto the Traveling Magician wrote the letter below to his twin sister Herberta. Since Humberto had to carry all his belongings on his back, he kept only one small sheet of paper and a short, stubby pencil in his canvas backpack. He used all the abbreviations he could to make his letter short.

Herberta could read her brother's letter easily, but their elderly mother had trouble. Help the poor lady out by circling each abbreviation and writing the word it stands for in the correct blank at the bottom of the page.

Dear Herberta,

   Tomorrow, Aug. 17, at 6:00 a.m., I leave for Prince Edward Is. In the Gulf of St. Lawrence, just N of Nova Scotia. I'm joining Dr. Hamilton and Mr. Snowden for a fishing trip on their 40-ft. boat. My address will be Capt. Hardy's Sea Inn, No. 12 Cedar St.

   Last mo. at the Claridge Apt., I met your old friend Loris. She's an atty. now for Greshem and Co. and likes her work. She came to my show at the Terrace Theatre on Green Ct. and enjoyed it, even though it lasted about an hr. longer than it should have. My magic rope got tangled up in Mrs. Quinto's hair, and then my rabbit fell into a gal. of buttermilk, so it took about 45 min. to get all that straightened out! But the audience loved it, and I'm doing another show there a wk. from next Sat.

   Hope all at our house on Grover Blvd. is fine and that you and Mom are doing all right without me this yr. I'll be home in Dec. Until then, write me c/o the Dept. of Magicians, Ottawa, Can.

Love from your devoted brother,
Humberto

a.m. _____

Sat. _____

Ct. _____

ft. _____

hr. _____

N _____

St. _____

Apt. _____

Can. _____

Dec. _____

gal. _____

mo. _____

Aug. _____

wk. _____

atty. _____

Capt. _____

Dept. _____

min. _____

Mrs. _____

Blvd. _____

Mr. _____

no. _____

Co. _____

Dr. _____

Is. _____

yr. _____

St. _____

c/o _____

Name: _____   Date: _____

Using Abbreviations

What's the Weather?

Find and circle 15 compound words in the cloud.
Words have been hidden horizontally, vertically, and diagonally, but never backwards.

Write the words on the lines as you find them.

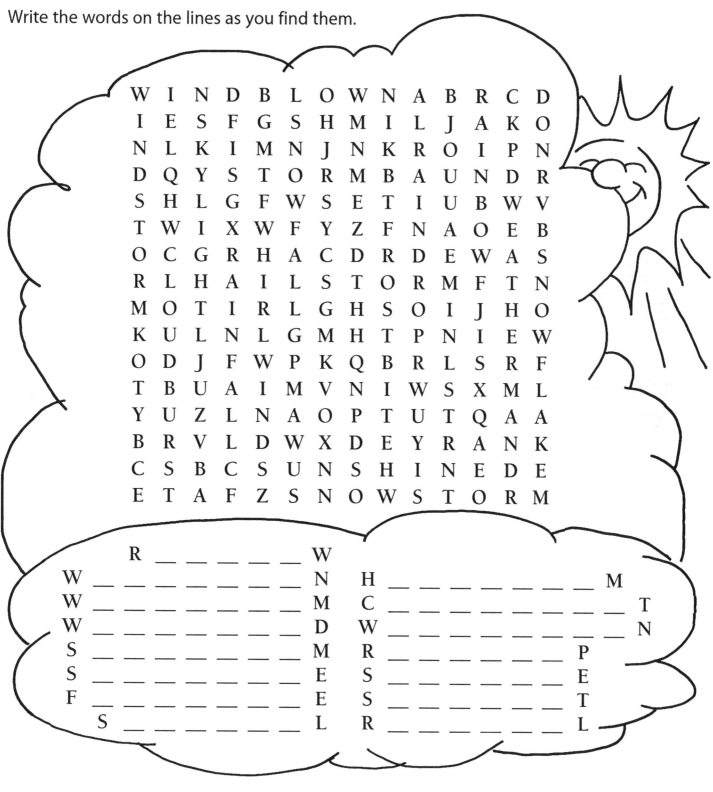

```
W I N D B L O W N A B R C D
I E S F G S H M I L J A K O
N L K I M N J N K R O I P N
D Q Y S T O R M B A U N D R
S H L G F W S E T I U B W V
T W I X W F Y Z F N A O E B
O C G R H A C D R D E W A S
R L H A I L S T O R M F T N
M O T I R L G H S O I J H O
K U L N L G M H T P N I E W
O D J F W P K Q B R L S R F
T B U A I M V N I W S X M L
Y U Z L N A O P T U T Q A A
B R V L D W X D E Y R A N K
C S B C S U N S H I N E D E
E T A F Z S N O W S T O R M
```

R _ _ _ _ _ _   W _ _ _ _ _ _

W _ _ _ _ _ _   N _ _ _ _   H _ _ _ _ _ _ _ _   M _ _ _ _ _

W _ _ _ _ _ _   M _ _ _   C _ _ _ _   T _ _ _ _ _

W _ _ _ _ _ _   D _ _ _   W _ _ _ _ _ _   N _ _ _ _ _

S _ _ _ _ _ _   M _ _ _   R _ _ _ _ _ _   P _ _ _ _ _

S _ _ _ _   E _ _ _   S _ _ _ _   E _ _ _ _ _

F _ _ _ _   E _ _ _   S _ _ _ _ _ _   T _ _ _ _ _

S _ _ _   L _ _ _   R _ _ _ _ _ _   L _ _ _ _ _

Name: _____   Date: _____

Language Literacy Lessons / Reading Intermediate

Copyright ©2002 by Incentive Publications, Inc.
Nashville, TN.

Using Compound Words

It's Not a Pretty Picture!

Write the story this picture tells.
Be sure to use capital letters and correct punctuation as needed.

_____

_____

_____

_____

_____

_____

_____

_____

Name: _____

Date: _____

Using Picture Clues

Language Literacy Lessons / Reading Intermediate
Copyright ©2002 by Incentive Publications, Inc.
Nashville, TN.

Thrifty Timothy Thorngill

Read the paragraph below all the way through.

Then write one of the words from the balloons in each blank to complete the sentences correctly.

Timothy Thorngill is a _____ teenager. He works hard to _____ of ways to save his money. But sometimes he does surprising _____ . Last Tuesday his uncle Thomas gave him _____ dollars to buy a fancy cake and ice cream to celebrate his _____ birthday. Timothy _____ of his brother and sister and decided to use the money to make them happy. Instead of buying the fancy treats, he used the money to purchase _____ tickets for his whole family. _____ he made popcorn and a _____ of lemonade and invited all the kids on the block to come _____ his party. _____ said _____ was a _____ kind idea and _____ Timothy profusely. Everyone said Timothy's _____ should be _____ setting.

think
thermos

they
this

trend
tremendously

thought
thrifty

thanked
thoughtfulness

things
thirty

theater
thirteen

then
to

Language Literacy Lessons / Reading Intermediate
Copyright ©2002 by Incentive Publications, Inc.
Nashville, TN.

Using Context Clues

Name:

Date:

Different Words, Different Story

Rewrite the story using the correct antonym from the box for each underlined word.
Give the story a surprise ending.

Words or phrases to use:

happy	soothing	harmless	quickly	downward	forward
quiet	young	strong	small	light	

As the <u>sad</u> <u>old</u> gnome <u>slowly</u> entered the forest, the moon cast a <u>dark</u> and <u>frightening</u> glow. Suddenly he heard a <u>loud</u> sound. Just then, he spotted a <u>dangerous</u>-looking vulture perched in a <u>huge</u> tree. As the gnome slowly moved <u>backward</u>, the vulture spread its <u>weak</u> wings and soared straight <u>upward</u>.

Name: _____

Date: _____

Recognizing and Using Antonyms

Language Literacy Lessons / Reading Intermediate
Copyright ©2002 by Incentive Publications, Inc.
Nashville, TN.

Mark the Homonym Trail

For years, the wicked wizard has been trying to steal Marilee Monster's jewels. After many close calls, Marilee decided to bury her jewels in the Homonym Desert. Since the wizard doesn't understand homonyms, Marilee decided that would be the safest place.

Marilee drew a map so her sister could find the jewels if she needed them, but her sister doesn't understand homonyms, either. Help Marilee's sister follow the maze (map) and find the jewels by writing in the correct homonym for the word written below the sentence on each sign.

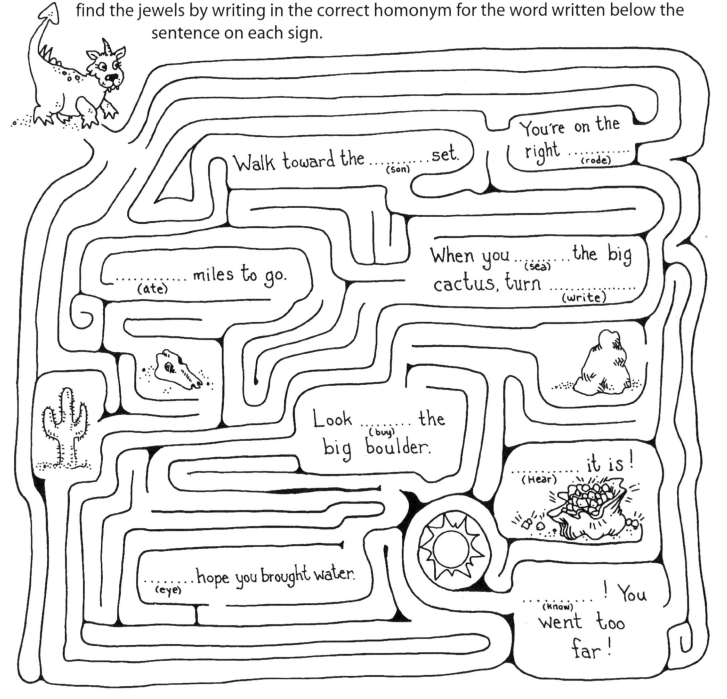

Walk toward the .... set. (son)

You're on the right .... (rode)

.... miles to go. (ate)

When you .... the big cactus, turn .... (sea) (write)

Look .... the big boulder. (buy)

.... it is! (Hear)

.... hope you brought water. (eye)

.... ! You went too far! (know)

Name:

Date:

Language Literacy Lessons / Reading Intermediate
Copyright ©2002 by Incentive Publications, Inc.
Nashville, TN.

Recognizing and Using Homonyms

Construction Ahead

Contractor Shibley is encouraging his crew to work furiously to meet the deadline for finishing the job on time. The problem is that the owner has specified that the foundation be completely built with bricks containing synonyms only.

Some of the bricks delivered by the brick-maker are defective. In addition to the synonyms, each brick contains a stray word.

Cross out the extra word on each brick to help get the job completed on time.

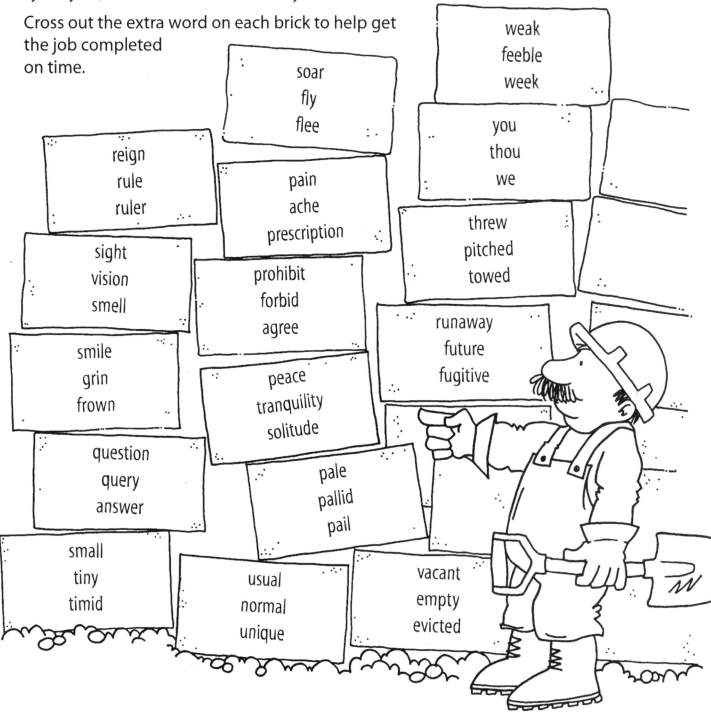

weak
feeble
week

soar
fly
flee

you
thou
we

reign
rule
ruler

pain
ache
prescription

threw
pitched
towed

sight
vision
smell

prohibit
forbid
agree

runaway
future
fugitive

smile
grin
frown

peace
tranquility
solitude

question
query
answer

pale
pallid
pail

small
tiny
timid

usual
normal
unique

vacant
empty
evicted

Name: _____

Date: _____

Recognizing and Using Synonyms

Language Literacy Lessons / Reading Intermediate
Copyright ©2002 by Incentive Publications, Inc.
Nashville, TN.

Sentence Sense

Combine 1 word or phrase from each of the 3 columns
to make sentences.

Words or phrases may be used more than once
as long as they are not used twice in the same sentence.

Over the rainbow	Terrific traffic jams	Sheds kindly light
Sprinkled with moonlight	Hordes of happy children	Triumphant
Always at midnight	The mermaid's cousin is	Glisten and gleam
Brighter than the sun	The unicorn was	Slinking past
Long, long ago	A huge lion	Regally proud
On a faraway shore	My favorite fairy tale	Roared mightily
On the mountaintop	A million stars are	Brightly beautiful
Across the miles	Icicle glitter is	Took place
This week	A full moon	Laugh and play
In the city	Sparkling raindrops	Frustrate and exasperate

1. _____

2. _____

3. _____

4. _____

5. _____

6. _____

7. _____

8. _____

9. _____

10. _____

Name: _____   Date: _____

Language Literacy Lessons / Reading Intermediate
Copyright ©2002 by Incentive Publications, Inc.
Nashville, TN.

Forming Sensory Impressions

Advice for Mike

Mike is packing his bags to leave for summer camp. His friends have all come to wish him goodbye. They have advice for him, too. They are giving it in figurative language, which means the message is a little different from what the words actually say.

On the line below each statement, write the meaning of the advice each of Mike's friends gives him.

Monty: For you, life at camp will be a breeze.

_____

Emily: You'll be on top of the world.

_____

Marta: It will be as easy as falling off a log.

_____

Joe: Be careful about blowing off steam.

_____

Blake: Don't get your dander up if you lose a race or two.

_____

Jean: By hook or crook, be a good camper.

_____

Jennifer: Don't blow your top if another camper disagrees with you.

_____

Gretchen: Don't get cold feet about asking questions.

_____

Julie: Hold your horses before you complain.

_____

Margaret: At the end of the summer, you'll be fit as a fiddle.

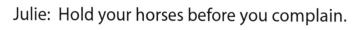
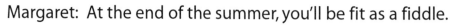

What is Mike actually telling his friends when he says, "I'll stay until the bitter end!"?

_____

Name: _____ Date: _____

Language Literacy Lessons / Reading Intermediate
Copyright ©2002 by Incentive Publications, Inc.
Nashville, TN.

More than You Wanted to Know About Butterflies

Write a sentence, and draw a picture to illustrate the sentence to explain the meaning of each of the following sayings.

Butterflies in your stomach

Valley of
the butterflies

Butterfly butter cookies

A butterfly kiss

Language Literacy Lessons / Reading Intermediate

Using Figurative Language

Copyright ©2002 by Incentive Publications, Inc.
Nashville, TN.

Say it Another Way

In the fewest words possible, write what you think
each of these sayings mean.

1. A little knowledge is a dangerous thing.

   _____

2. A penny saved is a penny earned.

   _____

3. Don't make a mountain out of a molehill.

   _____

4. I'm waiting for my ship to come in.

   _____

5. A bird in the hand is worth two in the bush.

   _____

6. Every cloud has a silver lining.

   _____

7. All that glitters is not gold.

   _____

8. Hold your horses.

   _____

9. Make hay while the sun shines.

   _____

10. Don't cry over spilled milk.

    _____

11. Keep your shirt on.

    _____

12. Don't count your chickens until they hatch.

    _____

Name: _____   Date: _____

Interpreting Idiomatic Expressions

Language Literacy Lessons / Reading Intermediate
Copyright ©2002 by INCENTIVE PUBLICATIONS, Inc.
Nashville, TN.

Pixie Power

Fill each blank below with the best descriptive word from the list. Use each word only once.

Words to use:

marvelous	evil	taller	bewildered	eerie	superstitious	mysterious
cunning	lonely	pudgy	unsuspecting	ruthless	mischievous	unfortunate
horrifying	flaming	confused	desolate	fastidious	frightened	alarming

1. Pixies are believed to be tiny, _____ fairies who have _____ red hair and pointed ears.

2. Pixies also have _____ faces and turned-up noses.

3. Legend has it that pixies love to mislead _____ travelers by causing them to become _____ and _____.

4. _____ travelers tricked by pixies can escape by turning their clothes inside out, as pixies are very _____ about dress.

5. Some travelers, _____ by stories of these _____ creatures, have been known to travel by day only.

6. Being trapped by pixies would be a _____ experience for a _____ traveler on a dark and _____ road.

7. Pixies have also been accused of being _____ and _____ horse thieves.

8. It is said that some _____ people even nail iron horseshoes above their barn doors to keep the _____ pixies away.

9. The tales about pixies become _____ and more _____ as they are passed down from generation to generation.

10. Even so, wouldn't it be a _____ experience to meet a pixie in all its _____ splendor?

Name: _____ Date: _____ (27)

Copyright ©2002 by Incentive Publications, Inc. Nashville, TN.

Using Descriptive Words

Word-Ability Wizard

Finding words in a bigger word is a game that helps people test their word ability.

Without using contractions, proper nouns, or slang, make as many words as you can from the letters in this word:

INVESTIGATION

To rate as a real word-ability wizard, find at least 40 words. Try to find 4-letter words, 5-letter words, 6-letter words and even some 7- and 8-letter words!

If you had fun with this one,
on a separate piece of paper try

PRESTIDIGITATION!!!

Date: _____

Language Literacy Lessons / Reading Intermediate
Copyright ©2002 by Incentive Publications, Inc.
Nashville, TN.

Comprehension and Independent Reading Skills

Up the Beanstalk

Climb the ladder with Jack!

Read Jack's story. Then fill in the **who, what, when, where, why,** and **how** ladder.

Although Jack meant to sell his mother's cow, he traded it for some bean seeds instead. When his mother threw the seeds out, they took root and grew into a tremendous beanstalk. Jack climbed it and found a giant's castle.

The wicked giant tried to kill and eat Jack, but Jack managed to escape down the beanstalk with the giant's treasures. The giant followed him, but Jack reached the bottom first, grabbed an axe, and chopped down the beanstalk. The giant crashed down into the earth with the beanstalk and vanished forever.

Jack and his mother kept the treasures and lived happily ever after.

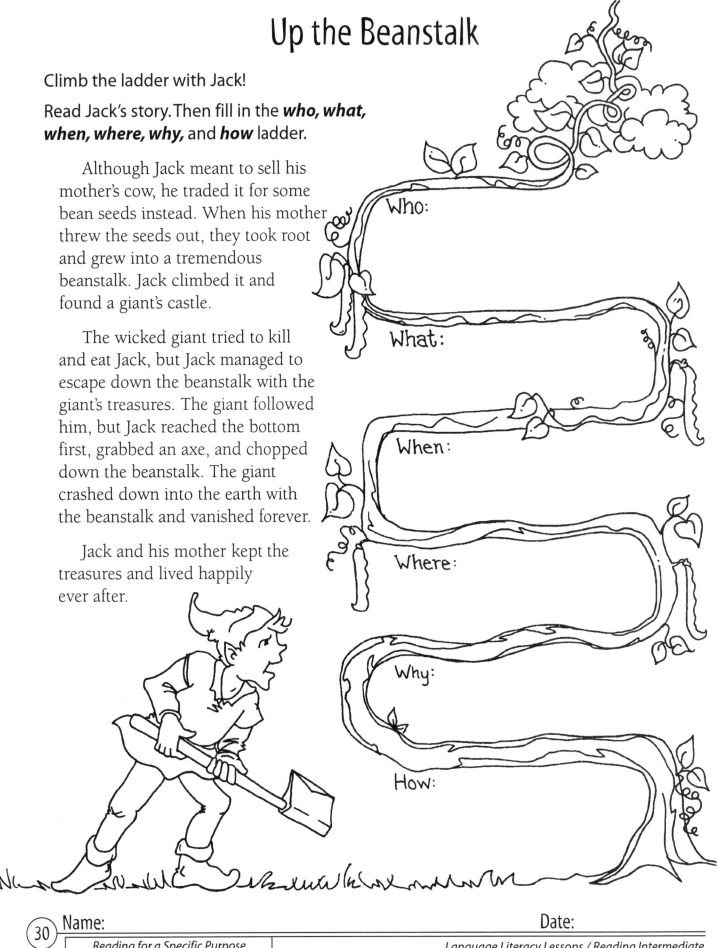

Who:

What:

When:

Where:

Why:

How:

Date: _____

Language Literacy Lessons / Reading Intermediate

The Knight's Journey

Read the story below. Underline the topic sentence in each paragraph.

The Silver Knight sat astride his faithful steed, his polished armor glinting in the sun. He had left the castle before daybreak on a mission for His Royal Majesty, King Peter the Peaceful. The message he carried was to be delivered to the King of Tarrn, for it was an invitation for the king and all his lords and ladies to attend a feast in celebration of ten years of peace between the two lands. By noon, the Silver Knight had crossed the border into Tarrn and was trying to decide which of the unmarked roads would lead him to his destination—the Great Hall of Tarrn.

Suddenly, he heard someone approaching on horseback. He closed his visor, raised his shield, and was ready to draw his sword. Although there was peace between the two countries, the Silver Knight knew there were many other dangers, such as thieves and cruel highway men, that made it necessary to use great care when traveling alone. Quietly guiding his horse off the pathway to the cover of a great old oak tree, the knight waited anxiously to discover the identity of the approaching rider.

Into the clearing before him emerged a splendid white horse, fitted with a halter of ostrich plumes and sparkling jewels. On the horse there sat a knight of the Great Hall of Tarrn. The Silver Knight could tell from the horse's fittings and the knight's shield that this was the king's own messenger. What could his mission be? The Silver Knight realized that this rider must be intending to deliver a message to his own King Peter! With this thought, he urged his horse forward into the clearing and approached the Knight of Tarrn with a smile and a palm upraised in a token of peace.

Name: _____

Date: _____

Language Literacy Lessons / Reading Intermediate
Copyright ©2002 by Incentive Publications, Inc.
Nashville, TN.

Identifying Topic Sentences

Goblins for Christmas

Read about the Christmas goblins.

Complete the sentences without reading the story again.
Then reread the story to check your answers.

Long ago, many people in Iceland told stories of the Christmas goblins. Children were told that the goblins appeared one at a time for 13 days before Christmas. The goblins were said to leave one at a time on each of the 13 days after Christmas. They were described as big and clumsy. People rushed around hiding Christmas goodies and making sure the house was goblin-safe. All sorts of spills, rips, and stains were blamed on these poor, ugly creatures. Storytellers say that many tales were told of the Christmas goblins, but not one person ever told of actually seeing one.

Circle the letter of the best answer.

1. The main idea of the story is
   a. Christmas goblins
   b. Christmas in Iceland
   c. How Icelandic children celebrate Christmas

2. The goblins were believed to stay in the house for
   a. 13 days
   b. 25 days
   c. 27 days

3. Stories of the Christmas goblins were
   a. True
   b. Half true
   c. Tall tales

Name: _____

Date: _____

Reading to Find Details

Language Literacy Lessons / Reading Intermediate
Copyright ©2002 by INCENTIVE PUBLICATIONS, Inc.
Nashville, TN.

Number, Please

Use the telephone directory to find a name and a telephone number to complete each sentence.

1. If I needed to have my teeth cleaned, I could call

   _____ at _____ .

2. To order a pizza and have it delivered to my house, I could call _____

   _____ at _____ .

3. If I am feeling lonely and need to talk to someone who will cheer me up, I can call

   _____ at _____ .

4. For emergency help, I could call _____

   _____ at _____ .

5. If I forget what my homework assignment is, I will call _____

   _____ at _____ .

6. If I need information to help me make vacation plans, I can call_____

   _____ at _____ .

7. When I want to talk to my best friend, I will call _____

   _____ at _____ .

8. If I need to have my bicycle repaired I can call

   _____

   at _____ .

9. If I needed information about when the post office is open,
   I would call _____

   at _____ .

10. If I need to find out the price of a new computer, I will call

    _____

    at _____ .

Name: _____   Date: _____

Language Literacy Lessons / Reading Intermediate

Copyright ©2002 by Incentive Publications, Inc.
Nashville, TN.

Reading to Find Details

Detail Selection

A few very important details have been left out of this story.

In each blank, write a word or phrase from the Detail Selection List.

Write **who, what, where, when,** or **why** next to each word or phrase from the list as it is used.

Then write 3 to 5 sentences to give the story a surprise ending.

Detail Selection List

strange adventure _____   large imagination _____

Timmy Thacker _____   hot day _____

muddy river bank _____   standing _____

_____ _____ was a young

boy with a very large imagination. If he had stayed home as

his mother told him to, he never would have been

_____ on that _____

_____ _____ on that

_____ _____ . It was because

of his _____ _____ that the

_____ _____ took place.

_____

_____

_____

_____

_____

_____

_____

Name: Date:

Reading to Find Details

Language Literacy Lessons / Reading Intermediate
Copyright ©2002 by Incentive Publications, Inc.
Nashville, TN.

Ballow's Dilemma

Read the sentences below.
Number them 1–9 to show the order in which they should appear.

_____ Angus told him that a coyote had been seen in the new pasture.

_____ Today the sheep would go to a new pasture.

_____ He was up and dressed before sunrise.

_____ Should he take a chance on moving the sheep today, or should he wait for the hunters to capture the coyote?

_____ This was the day that Ballow the shepherd had been waiting for.

_____ Angus also said that a party of hunters was searching for the coyote.

_____ With his lunch bag and stick, he headed for the pasture.

_____ With his heart beating furiously, Ballow tried to decide what to do.

_____ Along the way, he met his friend Angus.

Recopy the story in the proper sequence. Add a sentence to tell what Ballow decided to do.

_____

_____

_____

_____

_____

_____

_____

_____

_____

_____

_____

Name: _____   Date: _____   (35)

Arranging Ideas or Events in Sequence

How Does It End?

Read the sentences below.

Number them to show the order in which they should appear in the story.

Write 3 more sentences of your own to give the story a surprise ending.

_____ She had a lovely voice and took great pleasure in singing beautiful ballads as she worked.

_____ The daughter loved her father very much, but she longed for the friendship of people her own age.

_____ The old man was very sweet, but he was blind in one eye and completely deaf.

_____ Since her mother's death, the daughter had not been able to leave her father alone in the poor home in which they lived.

_____ Long ago in a land beyond the Sea of Sassafras, there lived a kind old man and his beautiful daughter.

_____ They lived mostly on fruits and berries from the forest, vegetables from their meager garden, and a few eggs from their hens.

_____ One day as she was singing in the garden, a handsome young man on a beautiful white horse rode up and asked for a drink of water.

_____ For many years they had not been into the village or talked with anyone except each other.

_____

_____

_____

_____

_____

_____

_____

Name: _____

Date: _____

Arranging Ideas or Events in Sequence

Language Literacy Lessons / Reading Intermediate
Copyright ©2002 by Incentive Publications, Inc.
Nashville, TN.

Storm Warning

Zerda and Gaslop were cruising along through space on their flight home. All was quiet on the Turasian spaceship, and Zerda was taking a nap as she sat beside the telecommunicator. Suddenly the machine flashed on, and the following information appeared on the screen.

You are approaching Sector VX6, Square #7 at 80,000 megaquarps per second, which will put you at the Sector border in 23.6 minutes. Although previously a neutral sector with light traffic and no weather, Sector VX6, Square #7 is now the center of a nuclear-ion tornado. Winds have been measured by monitoring equipment at 14,728.63 velosparks per second, which your ship is not equipped to handle. The force of the negative and positive nuclear ions has created a magnetic whirlwind, which is presently sucking in all spaceships in the surrounding vectors. We recommend that you summarize this information and feed it into your Skyway Path computer to set a new course away from the storm.

Summarize the information here so Zerda can plug it into the computer and get away from the storm.

_____

_____

_____

_____

_____

_____

Name: _____

Date: _____

Language Literacy Lessons / Reading Intermediate
Copyright ©2002 by Incentive Publications, Inc.
Nashville, TN.

Summarizing a Story

An Unhappy Trip

Read the story of the Parkers' trip.

In one or two sentences, state the reason the day turned out the way it did.

Then in one sentence, tell what they could have done to avoid the problem.

The Parker family had looked forward to a trip to Disney World for a very long time. They had saved money, packed their suitcases, and bought gas for the car. They had even carefully marked the road maps from their house to the motel where they would be staying. Just before dawn, they loaded the automobile, locked their front door, and got into the car. "Off to Disney World," they gleefully shouted. Everyone settled down for the long drive ahead and began to sing a song called "Away We Go." The Parker family loved singing together almost as much as they loved going to Disney World. The time passed quickly and soon they were at the entrance to the main highway leading directly to the park. Feeling very adventurous, the father, who was driving, proposed that it might be more fun to disregard the map and just take byways and unknown roads than to follow the less interesting super highways. This suggestion was met with enthusiastic support from the whole family. They liked exploring new roads and thought this was a great idea. After several interesting crooks and turns and an hour or two of driving, the roads began to be less tended and offered fewer markers. Trying to find locations on the map to match road signs became impossible. As the car sped on and on, the sun began to give way to a darkening sky and signs of a big storm on the way. Twists and turns, side roads and stretches of highway yielded no clue as to where the car was headed. Thunder, lightning, and pelting rain were not helping. Harmonious singing had long ago given way to quarreling and complaining, and the earlier happy mood had been replaced by anxiety and frustration. This would not be a day for the Parker family to remember as one of their best.

The reason the day turned out the way it did was _____

_____

_____

_____

What the Parkers could have done to avoid the problem was _____

_____

_____

Name: _____   Date: _____

Summarizing a Story

Language Literacy Lessons / Reading Intermediate

Let the Gnomes Know

Read all about the big celebration being planned for the gnomes.

Then help the gnomes by writing a short ad for the Gnomeville News. You may use only 3 sentences, so be sure to include only the most important information.

Six weeks ago, the Chief Gnome appointed eight gnome lieutenants to the planning committee for the Winter Moon Festival. Every Thursday night since then, the committee has met to work out the details of the celebration. They have decided to start the party at 10:00 p.m. next Friday night, the 13th of Gnovember, at Numb Skull Hill. All the gnomes in the gnomedom are invited and should wear costumes and bring musical instruments. First, second, and third prizes will be given for the ugliest costumes worn and the weirdest music made with an instrument. Prizes will be awarded at midnight by the Chief Gnome, and the king and queen of the festival will be introduced at that time also. Folk dancing, feasting and frolicking will follow these festivities until daybreak, when all good gnomes must be back underground.

Gnomeville News   page 24

COMING SOON!
Winter Moon Festival!

_____

_____

_____

_____

_____

_____

Name: _____

Date: _____

Language Literacy Lessons / Reading Intermediate
Copyright ©2002 by Incentive Publications, Inc.
Nashville, TN.

Summarizing a Story

What Next?

Finish the following picture sequences by "reading" them and drawing in your own conclusions.

Write a caption underneath each sequence to give it the best possible title.

Name:

Date:

Drawing Conclusions

Language Literacy Lessons / Reading Intermediate
Copyright ©2002 by Incentive Publications, Inc.
Nashville, TN.

World Travelers

Marta and Bob are world travelers. Last year they took a trip to Australia. Their plane departed from New York City, then landed in Oahu, Hawaii for refueling.

Since they had never been to New Zealand, they planned a stop-over in Auckland. Three days later, they arrived in Sydney, Australia with great expectations for what they would see and do there.

Trace Marta and Bob's journey on the accompanying map.
Then use the same map to plan Marta and Bob's return trip to the United States.

They will go by train to Melbourne, Australia and will conclude their international travel in Los Angeles, California.
To see as much as they can of the world, they would like to travel a different route and visit three different cities.

Pretend you are their travel agent and write their itinerary in the space below.

_____

_____

_____

_____

Name: _____ Date: _____

Language Literacy Lessons / Reading Intermediate
Copyright ©2002 by Incentive Publications, Inc.
Nashville, TN.

Reading and Using a World Map

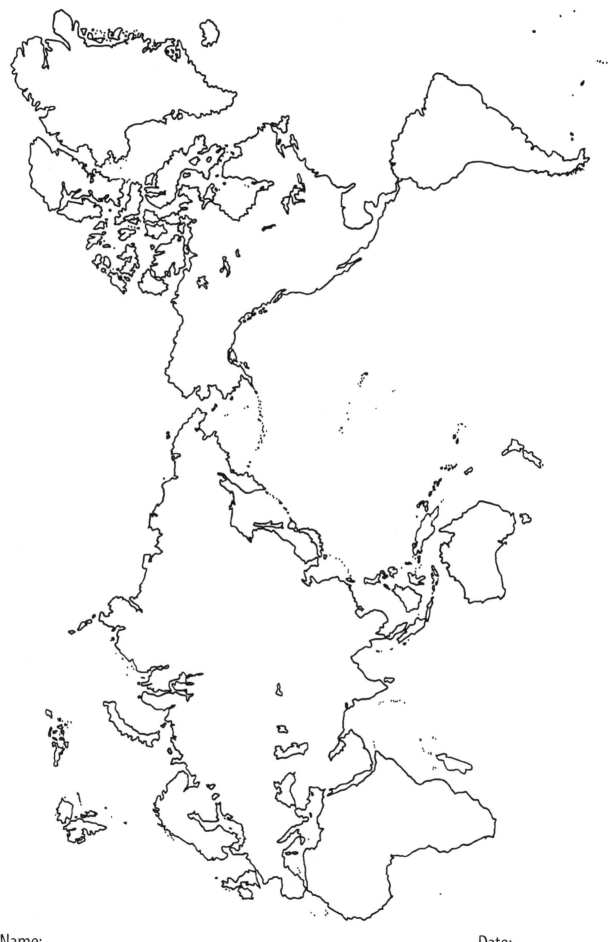

Name:

Date:

Reading and Using a World Map

Language Literacy Lessons / Reading Intermediate
Copyright ©2002 by Incentive Publications, Inc.
Nashville, TN.

A Time To Remember

Complete the story below to tell about Marta and Bob's stay in Australia.

From the time they stepped off the plane in Sydney, Marta and Bob knew this would be the trip to remember. Even the airport seemed alive with excitement and energy. As they exited the customs area and walked into the bright noonday sun, Bob pulled the map from his backpack, spread it out before Marta and they both breathed a deep breath of anticipation. Where would they go and what would they do first? It seemed too good to be true to finally be here in this long dreamed of country so far from home. Even in their wildest imaginations neither of them could ever have predicted the wild and unexpected adventure that lay before them.

_____

_____

_____

_____

_____

_____

_____

_____

_____

_____

Name: _____ Date: _____

Predicting Outcomes

Tell It Your Way

Write an ending for this story.

Once upon a time, a poor princess was lost in a forest. At nightfall a big storm blew up, and the princess tried to find some shelter. As she stumbled along in the rain, she suddenly saw a tremendous castle ahead. She ran to it and knocked loudly at the gate until the guards let her in.

The guards took her to the king and queen. She told them that she was lost and asked for help. The royal couple welcomed her and told her she could stay at the castle. She thanked them and went with the queen's lady-in-waiting to get some dry clothes.

During dinner that night, the princess met the son of the king and queen, who was home visiting his parents. They fell madly in love and immediately made plans to marry.

The only problem that they had to overcome was . . .

_____

_____

_____

_____

_____

_____

_____

_____

_____

_____

_____

_____

Name: _____ Date: _____

How Big is this Big Deal?

Read the ad that Bixie Big-Deal placed in the classified section of the Fairy Forest Newspaper.

Underline the sentences or phrases that you think are facts.
Circle the sentences or phrases that you think are opinions.

 **FAiRy FOREst NeWSPAPER** *page 27.*

CLASSiFiED ADVERTiSiNG

The brand-new Super-Duper Wand is now available at Treasure Troves, Inc., throughout the whole fairy kingdom. You must buy this fantastic, world famous, one-of-a-kind magic wand. This fabulous wand is rainbow-colored and folds to fit into a standard-size fairy knapsack. This wand is made of durable materials and is finely crafted. It comes with a lifetime guarantee. No self-respecting, ambitious young fairy can afford to go into the world without this wand.

The story has been told of the day the fairy wand saved the entire kingdom. Rumor has it that the king was so grateful that it was he who confirmed the name of Super-Duper Wand on the tool. It is said that the Treasure Troves that distribute the wand are actually owned by the royal family. Treasure Trove locations may be found throughout the kingdom. They are usually housed in small, but very attractive buildings.

It is believed that the Super-Duper Fairy Wand will ward off evil spirits, guard against unpleasant odors, and ensure the owner prosperity and good health.

RUSH to your nearest Treasure Trove Shop to buy your Super-Duper Fairy Wand today! Quantities are limited— tomorrow may be too late!!

CALL TODAY
TO PLACE
YOUR AD HERE!
1·800-777-1234

Name: _____

Date: _____

Read Before You Buy

Smart shoppers are label readers.

Read the paragraphs below, and complete the labels with factual information only. Include all important information, but omit opinions.

The sweater Mary wants to buy was hand-knit by a very old lady. They are the best sweaters on the market. The lady makes all her sweaters out of a pre-shrunk, all-wool yarn. All sweaters that she knits are beautiful. She uses only one pattern, which is a size 12, cardigan style. She reminds everyone to wash these sweaters by hand only. Hand washing will make them last for years.

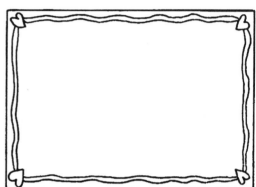

These oranges were grown in central Florida. They were ripened on the tree and were handpicked, packaged, and sold by the Ripe & Juicy Co. This company ships the best oranges in the world. The bag contains 12 oranges. Oranges are the best breakfast food in the country.

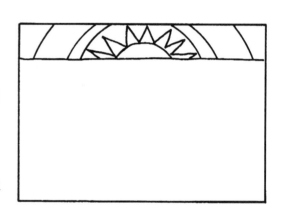

Joe has decided this backpack is the best buy of all the ones he has looked at. It is made of real leather, where the other ones have been made of synthetic materials. This one has adjustable straps and pockets with first quality zippers. It is lightweight, but very strong. It has six separate pockets to hold personal belongs securely as well as to make them readily available.

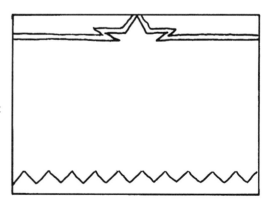

Name: _____

Date: _____

Distinguishing Between Fact and Opinion

Careless Clara Clark

The pictures in Column I show something that happened to Careless Clara Clark.
Each picture in Column II shows an effect of one of the happenings.

Draw a line to connect each "cause" picture with the correct "effect" picture.
Use the two empty boxes to draw your own set of cause and effect happenings.

Name:

Date:

Determining Cause and Effect

In the Mood

Here are some story excerpts in which the author tried to create a definite feeling or mood.

Read each one carefully. Identify the feeling or mood by drawing a line from the excerpt to the picture that shows the same mood.

Then reread each story and underline the key words (the ones that let you know the mood of the excerpt).

1. The beautiful princess began to look pale and miserable as each day she pressed her tear-stained face against the bar covering the tiny window of the dungeon where she was being held captive.

2. As the sun broke through the clouds and shed its brilliance over the tall trees and beautifully blooming vines, the whole forest took on a look of golden radiance.

3. The shoemaker could hardly believe his eyes when he awoke to find his whole shop filled with neat rows of carefully crafted shoes. The little store was spic and span, giving it an air of order and cheerfulness.

4. Prudence Porcupine did her very best to appear comfortable at the elegant table spread with glowing candles, sparkling crystal, and glittering silver. "If I can only eat without choking!" she thought to herself.

Write a paragraph of your own to show a feeling or mood. Draw a picture to illustrate the mood.

Then underline the key words just as you did in the previous excerpts.

5. _____
_____
_____
_____
_____
_____

Name: _____

Date: _____

Determining an Author's Purpose and Mood

Language Literacy Lessons / Reading Intermediate
Copyright ©2002 by Incentive Publications, Inc.
Nashville, TN.

Character Portraits

Put a name from the first column
with a description from the second column.

I	II
Sweet Susan	A kindly royal seamstress
Prince Charming	A shy shepherd
Lofty Leah	The good fairy
Sneaky Samuel	A naughty leprechaun
Leaping Lester	A sly troll
Rosebud	A happy gnome
Roly Poly	An enchanted princess
Meechum the Mighty	Ruler of a magic kingdom
Moonstar	A haughty queen
Timid Thomas	A handsome prince

Use each name and its matching descriptive phrase in a sentence.

Make your sentences tell something about the character of each individual. For example:
Rosebud, an enchanted princess, looked timidly out the castle window with gentle
thoughts and kind feelings for the hungry birds in the snow.

1. _____

2. _____

3. _____

4. _____

5. _____

6. _____

7. _____

8. _____

9. _____

10. _____

Name: _____   Date: _____   49

Finders Keepers

The pictures below represent characters dressed for a school play. Write a description of the role each person will portray.

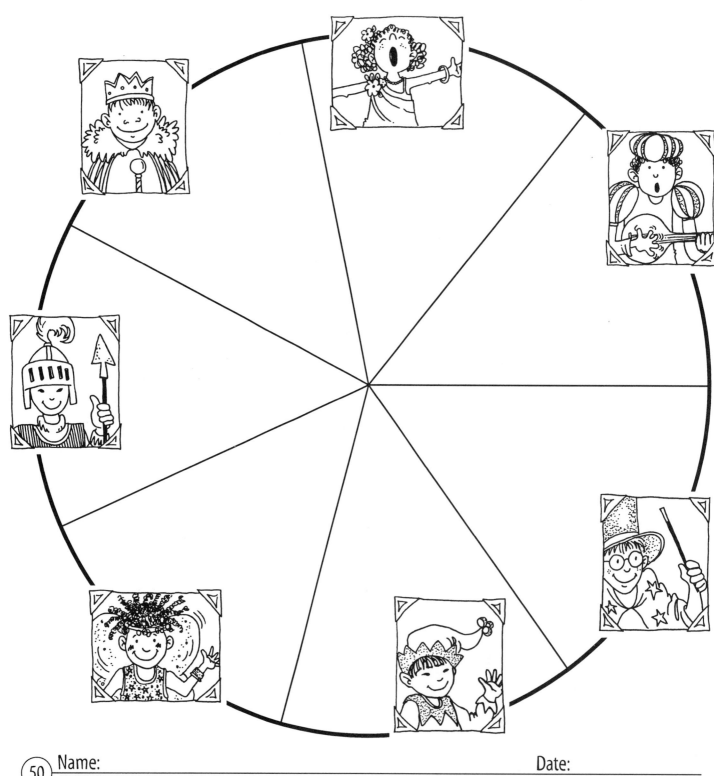

Name:

Date:

Identifing with Fictional Characters

Language Literacy Lessons / Reading Intermediate
Copyright ©2002 by Incentive Publications, Inc.
Nashville, TN.

Inside Story

If you could become a character in any book, what book would you choose?

_____

Why?

_____

_____

_____

_____

_____

How would your presence change the story
as you know it?

_____

_____

_____

_____

_____

_____

_____

_____

_____

Name 3 other books you have read of which you would like to be an actual part.

_____

_____

_____

Name 1 book whose story you would _never_ want to enter.

_____

Name: _____   Date: _____   (51)

Identifing with Fictional Characters

Reading Reflections

Think about all the books you have read, and reflect on each statement below before writing your responses.

1. Here is a three-line book review of a book I've just read.

   Title of Book: _____

   Author: _____

   Review: _____

   _____

   _____

2. If I were asked to recommend this book to a friend, I would say …

   _____

   _____

3. Right now, I am really interested in reading books about …

   _____

4. _____ is an author

   whose books I always enjoy. The thing I like best about books he/she has written is

   _____

   _____

5. _____ is a book that I didn't enjoy.

Name: _____   Date: _____

Extending Ideas from Material Read

Language Literacy Lessons / Reading Intermediate
Copyright ©2002 by Incentive Publications, Inc.
Nashville, TN.

The main thing I disliked about this book was _____

_____

6. If I could take only one book on a long journey, I would take _____

_____

because _____

_____

7. The book I would choose to share with a friend from another country would be

_____

because _____

_____

8. The most beautiful picture book I have ever seen in my whole life is _____

_____ . The illustrations are _____ .

9. If I could read a book about a subject I'm really interested in, see a video about the

same subject, or hear it narrated on audiotape, I would choose to _____

_____ because _____

_____ .

10. If I had a lot of money to buy books for presents, I would buy _____

_____ for _____

and for my own library I would buy_____

and for my best friend I would buy _____ .

Name: _____   Date: _____   53

Extending Ideas from Material Read

With Words in Mind

Certain words instantly bring pictures into your mind, just as certain pictures make you think of words that go with them. Can you combine words and pictures into a new art form?

Here is the way one person sees the word "dragon."

Now read these words, and draw your own pictures in the spaces below.

Sword	Knight
Princess	**Castle**

Name:

Visualizing Word Meaning

Date:

Language Literacy Lessons / Reading Intermediate
Copyright ©2002 by Incentive Publications, Inc.
Nashville, TN.

As You See It

Certain phrases automatically bring visual images to mind. These images are usually triggered by personal experiences and may be very different for any two people.

Read each phrase below, and quickly draw the very first picture that comes to mind. Ask a friend to do the same thing, and compare and discuss your finished drawings.

The end... ...of a perfect day	**"IN THE GROOVE"**
Up, up and away!	Sugar 'n Spice & Everything Nice
King of the Road	PACK UP YOUR TROUBLES

Name:

Date:

Visualizing Word Meaning

Organizing a Newsstand

The Ninth Street newsstand carries the 27 out-of-town newspapers listed below.

Help the customers find the newspaper they want by arranging them in alphabetical order by city.

Number the papers 1–27, and then write the correct name across the top of each paper.

_____ Pittsburgh Press
_____ Cleveland Plain Dealer
_____ Milwaukee Journal
_____ Boston Globe
_____ Atlanta Constitution
_____ Washington Post
_____ New York Times
_____ Chicago Tribune
_____ Saint Louis Post-Dispatch
_____ Los Angeles Times
_____ Nashville Tennessean
_____ Wall Street Journal
_____ Seattle Times
_____ San Antonio Express News
_____ Austin American-Statesman
_____ Los Angeles Times
_____ Dallas Morning News
_____ Tampa Tribune
_____ Charlotte Observer
_____ Baltimore Sun
_____ Houston Chronicle
_____ New Orleans Tribune
_____ Denver Post
_____ Phoenix Gazette
_____ Salt Lake Tribune
_____ Las Vegas Bugle
_____ Detroit Free Press

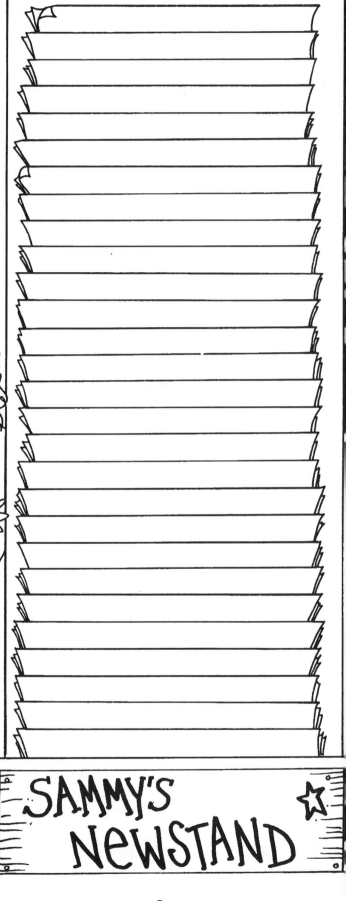

SAMMY'S NEWSTAND

Name: _____

Date: _____

Alphabetical Order

Language Literacy Lessons / Reading Intermediate
Copyright ©2002 by Incentive Publications, Inc.
Nashville, TN.

Author Under Investigation

Look up the word "author" in the dictionary.

Write the meaning in your own words. _____

_____

When we walk into a bookstore or a library and see rows and rows of books that we think we'd like to read, it is easy to forget that every single one of those books had to be written by a hardworking author.

Sometimes an author has to work for a long time before a book is finished. Other times, a book may be written in a short time. An author's life is in many instances unpredictable, and sometimes quite challenging.

1. Write the name of one of your favorite books. _____

2. Write the full name of the author. _____

3. Skim through the book and write a short paragraph to tell how old you think the author was and where you think he or she lived when the book was written.

_____

_____

_____

4. **Now conduct your research.** Ask your teacher or librarian to help you find reference materials to "find the facts" about the author. Write a short paragraph to summarize your findings.

_____

_____

_____

_____

5. Compare your 2 paragraphs. Were you
   _____ a. close to your guess?
   _____ b. amazed at the difference?
   _____ c. surprised?

Name: _____   Date: _____   57

Choose a Country

Select 1 of the countries listed below. Use at least 3 different resources (magazines, books, pamphlets, encyclopedias, atlases, etc.) to find the correct information to finish the sentences.

Thailand   Burma   Brazil

_____

(name of country chosen)

1. Two countries that border this country are

_____

_____ .

2. One of the most important industries of this country is

_____ .

3. The capital city is _____ .

4. Two important cities located in this country are

_____ and _____ .

5. The language spoken in this country is _____ .

6. Something that I found especially interesting about this country's

history is _____

_____ .

7. A major holiday of this country is _____ .

It is celebrated by _____

_____ .

8. This country <u>would</u> / <u>would not</u> *(circle one)* be an interesting vacation

destination because _____

_____ .

Name: _____   Date: _____

How Famous if Famous?

In the Question Box, write the name of a famous woman that you admire who is no longer living (athlete, author, world leader, humanitarian, other).

Use the encyclopedia to locate factual information about this woman.

How many paragraphs of information did you find about this woman? _____

Do you think the number of paragraphs
indicates how important or famous this woman was?_____

If you had been in charge of the encyclopedia, would you have included more, less, or
just about the same amount of information about this woman? _____

In what year was the woman born?_____

In what year did the woman die? _____

Why was the woman famous?_____

_____

_____

_____

Do you think the woman would become famous for doing
the very same thing if she were living now rather than then? _____

Name: _____   Date: _____

Language Literacy Lessons / Reading Intermediate
Copyright ©2002 by Incentive Publications, Inc.
Nashville, TN.

Using An Encyclopedia

The Humble Chef

Eaphraim is the best chef in all Elfland. He has served as chief chef for the great feasts of the most powerful kings, lords, and dukes in the land. In spite of this, he is a very humble elf. So humble, in fact, that when the Grand Duke asked him to prepare a list of his most famous dishes, the descriptions sounded dull and uninteresting.

Use a dictionary thesaurus to help Eaphraim find more colorful words to use to rewrite the descriptions.

Pecan and Honey Muffins: baked from wheat berry flour, clover honey, whole pecans, heavy cream, and eggs

_____

_____

_____

Mixed Vegetables: peas, carrots, and potatoes roasted slowly in the oven with fresh herbs and olive oil from Italy

_____

_____

_____

Green Salad: six different greens, picked fresh each day, mixed with tomatoes, cucumbers, and peppers before being sprinkled with salad dressing made from secret ingredients.

_____

_____

_____

Partridge in a Pear Tree Pie: chunks of meat and vegetables cooked together with special seasonings and baked into a pie

_____

_____

_____

Ruby-Berry Sparkle: ripe ruby-berries squeezed and strained and blended with spring water

_____

_____

_____

Snowflake Cream Torte: new snow mixed with cream and peach blossom nectar and churned until smooth and sweet

_____

_____

_____

Using A Thesaurus

Weighing an Elephant

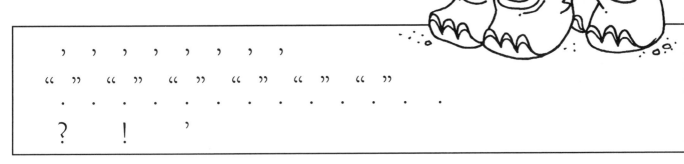

Read the story below and supply the missing punctuation.

Cross off each punctuation mark shown here as you use it.

Many many years ago a Chinese emperor was given an elephant by one of his loyal subjects Being a very curious emperor he immediately summoned his ministers

How much does this elephant weigh he demanded

, , , , , , , ,

" " " " " " " " " " " "

. . . .

? ! '

We do not know the ministers replied There are no scales large enough to weigh an elephant

A boy named Prince Chung had an idea I can weigh the elephant he announced calmly

Prince Chung led the elephant to a lake and coaxed the large animal in a boat Then he got into the water and painted a line on the boat just above the level of the water

The elephant clambered back to shore and Prince Chung filled the empty boat with stones until it sank to the painted line Then the stones were taken out and weighed When the weights of all the stones were added together Prince Chung knew the elephant s weight

You are very wise Prince Chung the grateful emperor said From now on you will be my respected friend

Name: _____

Date: _____

Running Errands

Chris was given a list of errands to run.

Using the map below, write the number found beside each errand into the correct block that shows where that errand will take Chris.

The first one is completed for you.
Be sure to follow the compass arrows.

Errand List

1. Lock the door of the house as you leave (southeast corner of 89th St. and 1st Ave.).

2. Go to newsstand and buy today's paper (west side of 1st Ave. north of 86th street).

3. Pick up shoes at shoe repair (southwest corner of 87th St. and 1st Ave., next door to newsstand).

4. Buy a tube of toothpaste at the drugstore (northeast corner of 87th St. and 2nd Ave.).

5. Stop by the laundry and ask how late they'll be open (northwest corner of 87th St. and 1st Ave.).

6. Go to bakery and have a treat (east side of 1st Ave. between 87th and 88th streets).

7. Stop at fruit stand and buy a basketful of strawberries (southwest corner of 89th St. and 1st Ave.).

8. Take paper, shoes, toothpaste, and strawberries back home (southeast corner of 89th St. and 1st Ave.).

9. Surprise! I'll treat you to a movie! Meet me at the theatre at 3:00 p.m. (southeast corner of 86th St. and 1st Ave.).

Map labels: 89th Street, 88th Street, 87th Street, 86th Street, 2nd Avenue, 1st Avenue. Block marked with "1".

Compass: N, S, E, W

Name:

Date:

The Enchanted Valley

Follow the directions below to break the spell and bring life back to the enchanted valley.

1. Draw a big, bright sun in grid B.

2. Draw two birds in flight in grid F.

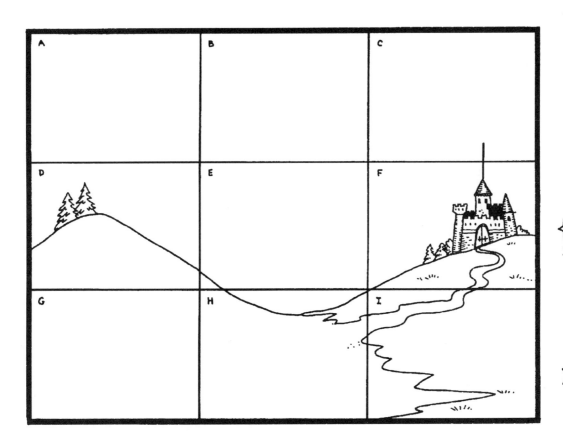

3. Put a small boat in the center of grid G.

4. Draw a puffy cloud in grid E and another in grid C.

5. Draw a lake in grid G and make it flow into half of grid H.

6. Put three more trees in grid D.

7. Fill grid I with pretty little meadow flowers.

8. Fly a flag from the castle.

9. Bring it all to life by coloring it!

Name: _____

Date: _____

Language Literacy Lessons / Reading Intermediate
Copyright ©2002 by Incentive Publications, Inc.
Nashville, TN.

Following Directions

Trolls in Trouble

If you read this story and follow the directions carefully, you will complete a beautiful picture. To make a wall poster for your room, just glue your finished picture onto a sheet of construction paper and hang it

Many years ago, the trolls who inhabited this beautiful forest retreat received some terrible news. A horde of cruel giants was invading the countryside, heading straight for their land. In desperation, they called on Mojo the Magician to help them. So Mojo cast a magic spell that removed all color and shape from the forest to hide it from the giants.

Through his art, Mojo knew that the giants would eventually be driven out of the forest. Using his magic powers, Mojo worked out a number code hoping that a hero would someday come along to restore the forest retreat. Until that time, the trolls and their forest would remain colorless and shapeless.

Can you help?

Use your crayons and this code to bring color and shape back to the troll's world shown on the next page.

If 6 x 9 = 54, color the #1 spaces purple.
If 5 x 8 = 40, color the #2 spaces brown.
If 7 x 4 = 28, color the #3 spaces red.
If 3 x 12 = 38, color the #4 spaces purple.
If 8 x 7 = 65, color the #5 spaces pink.
If 4 x 6 = 24, color the #6 spaces brown.
If 9 x 8 = 72, color the #7 spaces dark green.
If 12 x 3 = 36, color the #8 spaces light green.
If 11 x 6 = 66, color the #9 spaces pink.
If 8 x 6 = 48, color the #10 spaces sky blue.
If 11 x 10 = 101, color the #12 spaces tan.
If 7 x 5 = 35, color the #12 spaces dark green.
If 6 x 7 = 49, color the #14 spaces yellow.
If 12 x 5 = 60, color the #14 spaces yellow.

If 5 x 9 = 54, color the #16 spaces brown.
If 3 x 7 = 21, color the #17 spaces sky blue.
If 6 x 6 = 63, color the # 20 spaces pink.
If 9 x 9 = 90, color the # 20 spaces dark green.
If 12 x 10 = 120, color the # 20 spaces tan.

Name:

Date:

Name: _____

Date: _____

Language Literacy Lessons / Reading Intermediate

Following Directions

Outline Pin-Up

1. Write the name of a topic of interest to you above the pin-up line.
2. Think about what you want to know about this topic. Label each of the three line segments on the bedsheets with one of the main ideas you want to know about. (Example: Ireland—folklore; history; people)
3. Fill each bedsheet with information you learn about that sheet's main idea.

Name:

Taking Notes from Reading

Date:

Language Literacy Lessons / Reading Intermediate
Copyright ©2002 by Incentive Publications, Inc.
Nashville, TN.

Weather Watch

Read the sentences below.

Choose the best word to finish each sentence. Write the words in the correct spaces.

Words to use:

melt	closed	happy	memory	normal	approaching
dangerous	steadily	slowly	school	accidents	

All day, the weather station had reported an _____ storm.

The first snowstorm of the season came down softly but _____ .

By midnight, the roads will be _____ .

Because of the storm, schools will be _____ .

A school holiday will make the children _____ .

Buses and cars will move _____ .

There will be a good chance of many _____ .

Tomorrow the sunshine will cause the snow to begin to _____ .

In another day or two, the town will be back to _____ .

It will be back to _____ for teachers and students.

The unexpected vacation from school will become just a happy _____ .

Name: _____

Date: _____

Language Literacy Lessons / Reading Intermediate
Copyright ©2002 by Incentive Publications, Inc.
Nashville, TN.

Organizing Facts to Support a Conclusion

Behind Closed Doors

Just pretend . . . your teacher leaves the room. When the door closes behind her, it becomes completely stuck.

Everyone in the room tries to open it. The teacher, the principal, and the custodian try to open it from the hall, but cannot. Everyone, both inside and outside, tries to open the windows, but they are all stuck, too. The fire department and the police are summoned to rescue the students, but to no avail.

Finally, all signs of life outside the room cease.

The electricity in the room is off, it's dark, and only you and your classmates are left in the building. What will happen now?

_____

_____

_____

_____

_____

Name three of your classmates that you would expect to take over and offer a survival plan for the night?

1. _____

2. _____

3. _____

Of these three, whose plan would you expect to be most practical?

_____

Of these three, whose plan would you expect to be most creative?

_____

Which three of your classmates would you expect to provide entertainment to keep the class from panicking?

1. _____

2. _____

3. _____

Of these three, whose entertainment would you expect to be most successful?

_____

Of these three, whose entertainment would you expect to be most creative?

_____

On the back of your paper, give good reasons for each of your choices.

Name: _____   Date: _____

Personal Response to Material Read

Language Literacy Lessons / Reading Intermediate
Copyright ©2002 by Incentive Publications, Inc.
Nashville, TN.

What Would You Do?

If the door really did close on your classroom, and you and your classmates really were locked inside, and all the people on the outside were unable to help, what would YOU do?

Quickly write three sentences to tell what you would do.

1. _____

_____

_____

2. _____

_____

_____

3. _____

_____

_____

Number the sentences (1, 2, and 3) to show the order in which you would do them. Reread your sentences as ordered.

Does your plan make sense to you? _____ Is there something you left out or need to add? _____ If so, add it here.

_____

_____

_____

What person would you ask to help you carry out the plan? _____

Why? _____

_____

_____

Discuss your plan with someone whose judgment you trust. Ask for his/her suggestions, and for an opinion related to your plan's chance for success.

Name: _____   Date: _____ (69)

Shelve It!

Carefully read the list of book titles below.

Then follow the directions and write the title of each book on its proper shelf.

Titles

David Copperfield

A Wrinkle in Time

The Yellow Pages for Students and Teachers

Roget's International Thesaurus

Dictionary of American Slang

Webster's Dictionary

Grimm's Fairy Tales

Mainly Math

The Hobbit

Gardening for Young People

Oceans and Continents in Motion

Use that Computer!

1. On the blank books on the top shelf, write the titles of the books students would read for enjoyment.

2. On the middle shelf, write the titles of those books that would help students with their schoolwork.

3. On the bottom shelf, write the titles of the books students would use to find information on a specific topic.

Name: _____   Date: _____

Developing Appreciation and Reading Independence

Language Literacy Lessons / Reading Intermediate
Copyright ©2002 by Incentive Publications, Inc.
Nashville, TN.

Appendix

Reading Project Plan

Project Topic: _____

What I need to know: _____

Reading materials I will use: _____
_____

Project Plan

Time: _____

Gathering and organizing information: _____
_____
_____
_____

Activities: _____
_____

Plan for presenting my project: _____
_____

Evaluating my completed project: _____
_____

Language Literacy Lessons / Reading Intermediate
Copyright ©2002 by Incentive Publications, Inc.
Nashville, TN.

Library Lover's Law
or
The Nine Commandments for Library Lovers

Thou shalt not speak above a whisper—of all the treasures of the library, silence is golden.

Thou shalt remember to return or renew books and other materials before they are overdue.

Thou shalt not fold, spindle, or mutilate any materials from the library, but shall treat books with care and respect—they belong to everyone.

Thou shalt set out to learn where things are in the library, for knowing where to look is a valuable skill.

Thou shalt not let too much time pass without visiting thy library, for in the library thou wilt discover many wonderful things.

Thou shalt not reshelve books unless thou knowest exactly where they go. A misshelved book is a lost book.

Thou shalt not forget to tell thy friends about the good books thou hast read.

Thou shalt seek to expand thy interests and abilities by challenging thyself with good books.

Thou shalt take much pride in thy library, using and caring for what it has to offer.

Language Literacy Lessons / Reading Intermediate
Copyright ©2002 by Incentive Publications, Inc.
Nashville, TN.

Reading Record

Keep a record of your reading by writing titles of books as you read them.

Challenge a friend to a book race by trying to see whose bookshelf is filled first.

Fiction

History & Biography

Fantasy & Folklore

Language Literacy Lessons / Reading Intermediate
Copyright ©2002 by Incentive Publications, Inc.
Nashville, TN.

Fairy Tale Favorite

The name of my favorite fairy tale is

" _____ ."

This story is about _____

_____

_____

The setting of the story is _____

_____

The names of the characters are: _____

_____

The most interesting character in the story is _____ because

_____

_____

A summary of the plot of this story is: _____

_____

_____

I like this fairy tale better than the others I have read because _____

_____

_____

_____

_____

_____

Name: _____   Date: _____   75

Language Literacy Lessons / Reading Intermediate
Copyright ©2002 by Incentive Publications, Inc.
Nashville, TN.

Answer Key

Page 13

Prefixes and their root words:

disallow	intermission	rearm	rerun
disarm	international	reclaim	restate
disclaim	interplay	recount	retaste
discredit	interstate	redo	retie
dismission	misact	refit	unarm
dismount	miscount	relive	unclear
disobey	misfit	remission	undo
displace	misplace	remount	uneven
display	misplay	repack	unfair
distaste	prefit	repaint	unfit
interact	prepay	repay	unlace
interchange	prepack	replace	unpack
interlace	react	replay	untie

Page 14

Word	Suffix	Word	Suffix
act	ive	art	ist
deep	est	grace	ful
foo	lish	teach	er
patient	ly	good	ness
friend	ship	help	less
pay	ment		

Page 15

Phrases with contractions:
1. She doesn't know
2. They can't hear;
   It wasn't safe
3. Shouldn't she go;
   She'll know soon
4. I'm interested;
   Here's another story
5. She'll tell me;
   I'll never tell
6. There's treasure somewhere;
   They'll keep searching
7. She didn't remember;
   It's getting late
8. The tale's almost told
9. Here's the chest;
   You've guessed the secret
10. Gus couldn't swim
11. Who's there
12. Romeo's ready;
    It's never too late

Phrases with apostrophes showing possession:
1. The mermaid's fins;
   The ocean's floor
2. The waves' roar
3. Her mother's party
4. The boat's sail
5. The sea's secrets
6. The diver's work
7. Her friend's message
8. The sailor's question;
   Merry's answer
9. The gold's glitter
10. Geneva's blonde hair;
    Glen's laughter
11. The bottle's message;
    The sea's song
12. Julie's story

Page 16

abbreviation	meaning	abbreviation	meaning
a.m.	ante meridiem	atty.	attorney
Sat.	Saturday	Capt.	Captain
Ct.	Court	Dept.	Department
ft.	foot	min.	minutes
hr.	hour	Mrs.	Mistress
n.	north	Blvd.	Boulevard
St.	Street	Mr.	Mister
Apt	Apartment	No.	Number
Can.	Canada	Co.	Company
Dec.	December	Dr.	Doctor
gal.	gallon	Is.	Island
mo.	month	yr.	year
Aug.	August	St.	Saint
wk.	week		

Page 17

Words:

cloudburst	rainfall	sunshine
frostbite	skylight	weatherman
hailstorm	snowstorm	whirlwind
rainbow	snowfall	windblown
raindrop	snowflake	windstorm

Page 18

Answers will vary.

Language Literacy Lessons / Reading Intermediate
Copyright ©2002 by Incentive Publications, Inc.
Nashville, TN.

Page 19

Words in the order in which they appear in the story:
thrifty, think, things, thirty, thirteenth, thought, theater, Then, thermos, to, They, this, tremendously, thanked, thoughtfulness, trend

Page 20

word	antonym	word	antonym
sad	happy	dangerous	harmless
old	young	huge	small
slowly	quickly	backward	forward
dark	light	weak	strong
frightening	soothing	upward	downward
loud	quiet		

Page 21

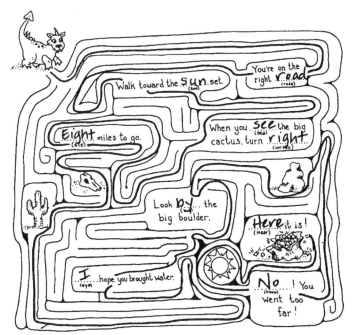

word	homonym	word	homonym
son	sun	buy	by
rode	road	know	no
ate	eight	eye	I
sea	see	hear	here
write	right		

Page 22

Words crossed out:

ruler	timid	solitude	we
smell	flee	pail	towed
frown	prescription	unique	future
answer	agree	week	evicted

Page 23

Answers will vary.

Page 24

Answers will vary; some explanations of the figurative language are:

Monty: For you, life at camp will be easy and natural; you won't have a difficult adjustment to camp life.

Emily: It will be one of the best times of your life; you'll be happy and enjoy a sense of freedom.

Marta: Camp will not be difficult or complicated.

Joe: Be careful about what you say to people; don't lose self-control in venting your frustrations.

Blake: Don't become irritated, defensive, or argumentative if you lose a race or two.

Jean: Use any and every means possible to remain a well-behaved camper.

Jennifer: Don't lose your temper, start a fight, or argue harshly if another camper disagrees with you.

Gretchen: Don't be afraid to ask questions; don't lose your courage for asking for directions and explanations.

Julie: Stop, calm down, and evaluate whether or not what you're about to say is helpful and encouraging before you complain.

Margaret: At the end of the summer, you'll be physically strong and capable.

Mike: I'm ready to go to camp and stay until the end of the summer, whether or not it's as wonderful as you all predict it will be.

Page 26

Answers will vary; some explanations of the sayings:

1. Knowing a few facts can lead someone to be arrogant and think he understands and can explain everything.
2. Each penny that is saved instead of wasted increases the amount of money someone has, which is like increasing his earnings.
3. Don't exaggerate a situation that's of little importance to one of colossal significance.
4. I'm hoping for and expecting something to happen, something lucky and wonderful that makes my life easier.
5. Something known or possessed for sure is better than something greater that is just a possibility and might never be owned.
6. There is something positive or redeeming in every difficult circumstance.
7. Something may appear valuable, worthy, or desirable while actually being cheap, worthless, or despicable.
8. Restrain yourself from acting hastily and rashly.
9. While conditions are favorable, get busy and accomplish what you need to do.
10. Don't spend your time worrying over and regretting unavoidable accidents.
11. Calm down; understand the entire situation before acting hastily and rashly.
12. Wait until you have seen the results before being confident in how something will turn out.

Page 27

Suggested answers given; adjectives may vary.

1. mischievous, flaming
2. pudgy
3. unsuspecting, bewildered, confused (order may vary)
4. Unfortunate, fastidious
5. frightened, mysterious
6. horrifying, lonely, desolate
7. cunning, ruthless

8. superstitious, evil
9. taller, alarming
10. marvelous, eerie

Page 28

(This list of 113 words is not exhaustive.)
2-letter: (10 total) to, so, on, no, at, it, in, is, as, an
3-letter: (27 total) gin, age, vat, ate, eat, tea, sit, tag, net, ten, tin, one, sin, tot, sat, son, van, tan, get, got, inn, ant, sag, gas, nit, not, ton
4-letter: (35 total) onto, into, goat, gone, tone, tine, neat, gate, nest, vent, vein, vane, stain, test, tent, gnat, sage, seat, nine, noes, sang, song, sing, tang, sane, gain, gait, gist, sent, tint, gave, give, note, vote, nave
5-letter: (10 total) tinge, state, stone, stage, sting, stove, stave, agate, agave, taste
6-letter: (11 total) attend, nation, invest, invent, ingest, seven, tonnage, toning, eating, voting, noting
7–8 letter: (19 total) station, invitation, negation, vegetation, gestation, instigate, instant, getting, stoning, seating, sitting, inviting, nesting, testing, staining, venting, netting, stating, tasting

Page 30

(Wording will vary)
Who: Jack
What: steals treasure from a giant's castle and then causes the giant's death
When: after Jack's mother threw the bean seeds outside
Where: up the beanstalk that grew from the bean seeds
Why: Jack wanted the giant to fall because the giant had attempted to kill and eat the invader who stole his treasure
How: chopped down the beanstalk

Page 31

Topic Sentences:
He had left the castle before daybreak on a mission for His Royal Majesty, King Peter the Peaceful.
Suddenly, he heard someone approaching on horseback.
On the horse there sat a knight of the Great Hall of Tarrn.

Page 32

1. a   2. a   3. c

Page 33

Answers will vary.

Page 34

strange adventure	what	large imagination	why
Timmy Thacker	who	hot day	when
muddy river bank	where	standing	how

Timmy Thacker was a very small boy with a very large imagination. If he had stayed home as his mother told him to, he never would have been standing on that muddy riverbank on that hot day. It was because of his large imagination that the strange adventure took place.

Page 35

Order of numbers going down the page: 6, 2, 3, 9, 1, 7, 4, 8, 5
Story with sentences correctly ordered:
1. This was the day that Ballow the shepherd had been waiting for.
2. Today the sheep would go to a new pasture.
3. He was up and dressed before sunrise.
4. With his lunch bag and stick, he headed for the pasture.
5. Along the way, he met his friend Angus.
6. Angus told him that a coyote had been seen in the new pasture.
7. Angus also said that a party of hunters was searching for the coyote.
8. With his heart beating furiously, Ballow tried to decide what to do.
9. Should he take a chance on moving the sheep today, or should he wait for the hunters to capture the coyote?

Page 36

Order of numbers going down the page: 7, 6, 5, 3, 1, 2, 8, 4
Story with sentences correctly ordered:
1. Long ago in a land beyond the Sea of Sassafras, there lived a kind old man and his beautiful daughter.
2. They lived mostly on fruits and berries from the forest, vegetables from their meager garden, and a few eggs from their hens.
3. Since her mother's death, the daughter had not been able to leave her father alone in the poor home in which they lived.
4. They had not been into the village or talked with anyone but each other for many years.
5. The old man was very sweet, but he was blind in one eye and completely deaf.
6. The daughter loved her father very much, but she longed for the friendship of people her own age.
7. She had a lovely voice and took great pleasure in singing beautiful ballads as she worked.
8. One day as she was singing in the garden, a handsome young man on a beautiful white horse rode up and asked for a drink of water.

Pages 41–42

Itinerary: answers will vary.

Page 45

Facts are underlined, opinions are in bold. (Some sentences can be argued to be both/either fact and/or opinion. These sentences are underlined *and* in bold.)

The brand-new, Super-Duper Wand is now available at Treasure Troves, Inc., throughout the whole fairy kingdom. **You must buy this fantastic, world famous, one-of-a-kind magic wand.** This fabulous wand is rainbow-colored and folds to fit into a standard-size fairy knapsack. This wand is made of durable materials and is finely crafted. It comes with a lifetime guarantee. **No self-respecting, ambitious young fairy can afford to go into the world without this wand.**

The story has been told of the day the fairy wand saved the entire kingdom. Rumor has it that the king was so grateful that it was he who confirmed the name of Super-Duper Wand on the tool. It is said that the Treasure Troves that distribute the wand are actually owned by the royal family. Treasure Trove locations may be found throughout the kingdom. They are usually housed in small but very attractive buildings.

Language Literacy Lessons / Reading Intermediate
Copyright ©2002 by INCENTIVE PUBLICATIONS, Inc.
Nashville, TN.

It is believed that the Super-Duper Fairy Wand will ward off evil spirits, guard against unpleasant odors, and ensure the owner prosperity and good health.

RUSH to your nearest Treasure Trove Shop to buy your Super-Duper Fairy Wand today! Quantities are limited—tomorrow may be too late!

Page 46

Important information:

Sweater: hand-knit; pre-shrunk, all-wool yarn; size 12; cardigan style; hand wash only

Oranges: grown in central Florida; tree-ripened; handpicked, packaged, and sold by the Ripe & Juicy Co.; 12 oranges in the bag

Backpack: real leather; adjustable straps; pockets with zippers; lightweight; six separate pockets

Page 47

Page 48

Page 56

Papers listed in alphabetical order:

1. Atlanta Constitution
2. Austin American-Statesman
3. Baltimore Sun
4. Boston Globe
5. Charlotte Observer
6. Chicago Tribune
7. Cleveland Plain Dealer
8. Dallas Morning News
9. Denver Post
10. Detroit Free Press
11. Houston Chronicle
12. Las Vegas Bugle
13. Los Angeles Daily Journal
14. Los Angeles Times
15. Milwaukee Journal
16. Nashville Tennessean
17. New Orleans Tribune
18. New York Times
19. Phoenix Gazette
20. Pittsburgh Press
21. Saint Louis Post-Dispatch
22. Salt Lake Tribune
23. San Antonio Express News
24. Seattle Times
25. Tampa Tribune
26. Wall Street Journal
27. Washington Post

Page 58

Thailand

1. Burma, Malaysia, Kampuchea, Laos
2. Agriculture (rice); Rubber; rice milling; tapioca clipping, and more
3. Bangkok
4. Bangkok, Chiang Mai, Nakhon Ratchasima
5. Thai
6. Answers will vary.
7. Answers will vary.
8. Answers will vary.

Burma

1. Thailand, Laos, China, India, Bangladesh
2. Farming (rice), forestry, mining
3. Rangoon (or Yangon)
4. Rangoon (or Yangon), Mandalay, Moulmein, Thaton, Myingyan, Meiktila, Pakokku, Sittwe, Prome, Toungoo, Henzada, Pegu
5. Burmese
6. Answers will vary.
7. Answers will vary.
8. Answers will vary.

Brazil

1. Guyana, French Guiana, Suriname, Venezuela, Colombia, Peru, Bolivia, Paraguay, Argentina, Uruguay
2. agriculture (coffee, cacao, sugarcane); forestry; manufacture of rubber
3. Brasilia
4. Brasilia, Sao Paulo, Rio de Janeiro, Recife, Salvador, Fortaleza, Belo Horizonte, Porto Alegre
5. Portuguese
6. Answers will vary.

7. Carnival—for the four days before Lent, all of Rio de Janeiro closes business for costume receptions, balls, contests, parties, and parades in the streets.
8. Answers will vary.

Page 61

Correctly punctuated story:

Many, many years ago a Chinese emperor was given an elephant by one of his loyal subjects. Being a very curious emperor, he immediately summoned his ministers.

"How much does this elephant weigh?" he demanded.

"We do not know," the ministers replied. "There are no scales large enough to weigh an elephant."

A boy named Prince Chung had an idea. "I can weigh the elephant," he announced calmly.

Prince Chung led the elephant to a lake and placed the large animal in a boat. Then he got into the water and painted a line on the boat just above the level of the water.

The elephant was removed, and the boat was filled with stones until it sank to the painted line. Then the stones were taken out and weighed. When the weights of all the stones were added together, Prince Chung knew the elephant's weight.

"You are very wise, Prince Chung," the grateful emperor said. "From now on you will be my respected friend!"

Page 62

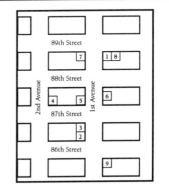

Page 70

1. Enjoyment shelf: David Copperfield, A Wrinkle in Time, Grimm's Fairy Tales, The Hobbit
2. Schoolwork shelf: Roget's International Thesaurus, Dictionary of American Slang, Webster's Dictionary, Mainly Math
3. Information shelf: The Yellow Pages for Students and Teachers, Gardening for Young People, Oceans and Continents in Motion, Use that Computer!

Language Literacy Lessons / Reading Intermediate
Copyright ©2002 by Incentive Publications, Inc.
Nashville, TN.